D1733514

EVERYTHING I KNOW
I LEARNED AT
THE MOVIES

A Compilation
Of Clichés And Un-Truisms
Gleaned From A Lifetime Spent
Entirely Too Much In The Dark

By JOHN JB WILSON

GENERAL PUBLISHING GROUP

Los Angeles

Publisher: W. Quay Hays
Managing Editors: Colby Allerton, Peter Hoffman
Art Director: Kurt Wahlner
Production Director: Nadeen Torio
Color and Prepress Director: Gaston Moraga
Production Assistants: Alan Peak, Tom Archibeque

© 1995 by John JB Wilson

For information:
General Publishing Group, Inc.
2701 Ocean Park Boulevard
Santa Monica, CA 90405

Library of Congress Catalog Card Number: 95-081314
ISBN: 1-881649-64-4

Printed in the USA
10 9 8 7 6 5 4 3 2 1

General Publishing Group
Los Angeles

To BARBARA JEAN...
The Best Thing
I Ever Found
at The Movies.

ACKNOWLEDGMENTS

To the countless friends, family members, fellow movie buffs (and total strangers) who offered me their feedback, suggestions, support and time in putting this book together: My heartfelt thanks. Now, for the hard part... remembering all the important names, and not forgetting anyone who deserves inclusion. My apologies in advance to anyone I've overlooked.

For her endless support, input and indulgence of me, I must first acknowledge my wife and life partner: Barbara, you helped me with this book in ways you may not even know. To Tom Higgins, Allison Jackson and little Spencer (and even Baby Jackson!)—I will always owe a special debt of gratitude for your being best friends in every sense. To my parents and brothers—who were my first audience and most supportive critics—I see the humor in the whole experience, and hope you do, too.

To Dan Campbell, Bill Hall, Nancy Lilienthal, Kelie McIver, Mo Murphy, Micki Sackler (and the rest of The RAZZberry Gang!)—thanks for encouraging and participating in my dreams. To Alan, Cheryl, Irving, Larry, Patti, Maxine and Murray (not The Andrews Sisters, but just as enjoyable to listen to!)—my appreciation for keeping me grateful, and steering me onward. To Sarah Fuller, my thanks for your generosity in absentia. To Robert Simons, whose computer expertise saved this project from the edge of the abyss: good work, man! To Robert Cosenza at The Kobal Collection: your contributions were "picture perfect." And to my agent Michael Hamilburg (and his sweet-voiced sidekick Joanie!), my publisher Quay Hays (and his terrific staff) who saw this book's potential (and jumped on it in record time!): This could never have happened without you.

FOREWORD

Like many people born after 1950, I've spent a great part of my life with The Movies—seeing them in theatres, watching them on television and, more recently, renting them on video. When I was younger, I took everything they told me at face value: I honestly believed that what happened on screen reflected REAL life.

Some of what this taught me was perfectly harmless: the idea that Doris Day really was a virgin at 40... that Rock Hudson wanted nothing more than to get Doris into the sack... that Elvis Presley, with one un-plugged electric guitar on a backlot Hawaiian beach, could actually create the sound of an entire studio recording session...

But some of what this taught me—much of what's in this book—had the potential to really get me in trouble. If I measured myself against movie heroes and movie stars, I would almost always come up short. If I measured the arc of my life against the plot of the average 1930's M-G-M picture, it was sorely lacking in adventure, intrigue and romance. And if I measured my own happiness against that of the lives passing gleefully, glamorously by me on the silver screen, I could easily build a case for ending it all...

Luckily for me, my wife, our soon to be born child and the publishers of this book, I did not. Instead, I learned to take The Movies' version of life with a grain of celluloid—to laugh at the gargantuan gap between "reel" life and REAL life.

And that, as they say, is how this book was born. It grew out of a lifelong love of movies... and out of a sarcastically adult perspective on both my own genuine naïveté, and the manufactured naïveté of those hundreds of actors, screenwriters, directors and movie technicians whose sole purpose in life sometimes seemed to be showing the rest of us just how humdrum our real lives really are.

Hum-drum or not, today I am grateful. For the sense of humor that produced this book. For the efforts on the part of General Publishing Group to bring it to market. For the love of my wife and family. And, believe it or not, for the fact that my swash, to this day, has yet to be buckled—and the fact that I now know... it doesn't necessarily need to be.

John JB Wilson
July 25, 1995

No Problem Is So Big It Can't Be Solved in 12 Reels

(Or Less!)

Everyone Else
Looks Simply
STUNNING
First Thing
in
the Morning.

EVERYONE

(Except YOU!)

Has a GREAT SEX LIFE!

The Happiest Couples Sleep in Twin Beds.

THE NATIVES ARE ALWAYS RESTLESS!

Neither Fire,
Flood,
Famine
nor
Earthquake
Can Affect
The Leading Lady's
PERFECT
Hair and Make-Up.

NOTHING Can Ruin Your Life Like MONEY

BATHTUBS EXIST ONLY AS AN EXCUSE FOR GRATUITOUS NUDITY.

Scintillating
Conversation
Naturally Flows
from
Most People's
Lips.

"PSYCHO" 9401
DIR. MR. HITCHCOCK
CAM. J. RUSSELL
1-29-60 DAY
TR8 6

IF YOU BLOW YOUR LINES, THERE'S ALWAYS ANOTHER TAKE

Once People
Get to Know You,
You'll Forever
Be Typecast
as

COMIC,

Tragic

or

MUSICALLY
TALENTED

HOLLYWOOD Has Movie Stars on Every Street-Corner.

If You Don't Know
How to Play
a Musical Instrument,
Someone Else's Hands
Can Be Hired
for
The Close-Ups.

MOST OF LIFE'S PROBLEMS CAN BE SOLVED...

BY SINGING AND DANCING!

When The Star
Breaks Her Leg
15 Minutes
Before The
Opening Night Curtain,
<u>ANYBODY</u>
Can Learn
Her <u>Entire</u> Part
In
14 Minutes
—OR LESS!

Truly Great Composers Can Write a Classic in Two Minutes

(45 Seconds If There's a Montage!)

INVENTING SOMETHING TAKES PLENTY OF HARD WORK...

(BUT VERY LITTLE ACTUAL SCREEN TIME)

To Properly
Tell Someone
About
a Dream,
**Special
Visual Effects**
Are Required.

Prostitution Is a REWARDING Career Choice...

...And a Great Way to Meet Men!

NUNS

Are Secretly Fun– Loving Chicks!

Precocious Children Are a Joy to Behold

All
Grandparents
Are
Wise
and
Kind

ALL
FATHERS
ARE
GOOD
LISTENERS

MOTHER

ALWAYS

KNOWS

BEST!

HEROES

NEVER

FLINCH

Anyone
with A Scar
on His Face
MUST
Be
A Bad Guy.

**From Every Building
on
Every Street
in The Entire City
of**

Paris,

**You Can
Clearly See
The
Eiffel Tower...**

From
Every Window
of
Every Office
in
Every Building
in
Washington D.C.
You Can Clearly See
The Capitol Dome...

From Every Window
In Every Room
(On Every Floor)
Every Guest
Can Clearly See
The Neon Sign
Endlessly Flashing:

HOTEL...
HOTEL...
HOTEL...

The Fastest Way to Travel is By Montage.

When
Airplanes
Fly
Around
The World,
Giant
Connect-
The-Dots
Lines
Follow
Behind Them.

MEN ONLY WANT ONE THING!

WOMEN
Who Enjoy
SEX
ARE
CHEAP!

A Woman Can't Win a Man Without Resorting to Trickery

Marriage

Should

Always

Occur

Before

Sex

THE KILLER WILL ALWAYS CONFESS AT THE LAST MINUTE...

(AND CLEARLY EXPLAIN HIS MOTIVE WITH HIS DYING BREATH!)

CRIMINALS ALWAYS RETURN TO THE SCENE OF THE CRIME

**The Fastest Way
to Solve a Murder
is to Gather
All of the Suspects
in One Room
and Grill Them
Relentlessly,
Until One of Them
Pulls a Weapon—
or Confesses!**

INNOCENT PEOPLE DO NOT HAVE (Or Need) ALIBIS

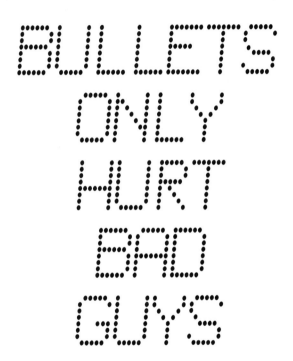

BULLETS
ONLY
HURT
BAD
GUYS

A SIX-SHOOTER CAN HOLD SEVEN BULLETS
(OR MORE!)

Before Firing
The Gun He Has
Aimed Right at You,
The Bad Guy
Will Take a Moment
To Explain
Why He Went Bad—
Thus Giving You
Just Enough Time
to
Gain The Upper Hand!

All It Takes
to
Dig
Your Way
Out of Prison
is
A Soup Spoon

(and a Lot
of Patience!)

With Enough Packs of Smokes, A Prisoner Can Get ANYTHING In The World.

The Executioner Will Have His Hand On The Switch Before The Governor Calls With a Pardon

MOST MIRACLES ARE JUST SPECIAL EFFECTS.

GOD

*has a voice
exactly like
Cecil B. DeMille's . . .*

The Bible

IS CHOCK-FULL
OF
REVELRY, RIBALDRY
AND
WORLD-CLASS
CAROUSING

(ALL OF WHICH IS,
OF COURSE,
PUNISHED IN THE END!)

The White Man Won The West FAIR and SQUARE

INDIANS
ARE JUST
WHITE
PEOPLE
IN
MAKE UP
AND
BAD WIGS

THE ONLY FEMALES IN THE OLD WEST WERE SCHOOL MARMS AND SALOON GIRLS

NOBODY

in a

BLACK HAT

is

EVER

up to

ANY GOOD.

SMART WOMEN ARE MORE TROUBLE THAN THEY'RE WORTH!

SCIENTISTS
ARE
USUALLY

Street
Urchins
Are
Always
Adorable

REAL MEN STRIKE FIRST...

(And Don't Bother To Ask Questions Later!)

Women Are Useless When a Fight Breaks Out

(Unless There's a Bottle
—Or Other Breakable Object—
Nearby...)

A
WOMAN
WHO
KNOWS
WHAT
SHE
WANTS
IS
DANGEROUS!

EVERYONE
Smokes a
Cigarette
After
Sex

DRUNKS Are Fun People to Know

Crazy People
are always
CRAZY
in
Obvious
Ways

FAT PEOPLE
Are
Only Good
for
COMIC
RELIEF.

MONSTERS

ARE EASY
TO SPOT...
THEY LOOK
LIKE
BORIS KARLOFF
AND TALK
LIKE
BELA LUGOSI

Whenever An Angry Mob Assembles in The Town Square, Everyone Knows to Bring Their Own Torch!

THE VILLAGE IDIOT

Is a Veritable Font of Wisdom

Nubile Young Women
Simply
Do Not Understand
The Perils
of
Entering
Haunted Houses
Alone.

Gorgeous
Young Women
Find
Aging Men
Completely
IRRESISTIBLE...

…But Aging Women Involved with Attractive Younger Men Are Always PATHETIC!

THE HOLIDAYS ARE A JOYOUS TIME FOR EVERYONE

Life Is Much More Interesting in TECHNICOLOR®

Well-Adjusted People Have Answers for _Everything_

"B"
MOVIE STARS
MAKE
EXCELLENT
GOVERNORS,
SENATORS
AND
PRESIDENTS.

If You're
The Good Guy,
Even with
100 Guns Aimed
Right at
Your Head,
98 of Them
Will Miss

*(And The Two That DO Hit You
Will Result in
Only Minor Flesh Wounds!)*

**When Shot
in The Back at
Point Blank Range,
The Hero
Will Survive—
But Only Long Enough
to Deliver
a Poignant
(Some Might Even Say
Long-Winded)
Monologue.**

After You Reach A Certain Age, You Will Only Be Offered Character Parts and Horror Movie Roles.

The THICKER The Accent, The GREATER The Performance

When You Are
Unexpectedly Asked to Sing
At a Swank Society Party,
The Orchestra Leader
(Whom You've Never Met)
Will Intuitively Know
The Exact Key, Tempo
and Arrangement
of The Song
You Extemporaneously
Decide to Perform—
Even if the Song
Has Never Been Heard
Anywhere Before.

When Driving Down
A Winding Mountain Road
While Carrying On
A Conversation,
Always Remember:
It Is More Important to
Maintain Eye Contact
With Your Passenger
Than to Look At
The Road
In Front of You.

THERE IS NO LIFE CRISIS THAT A GOOD CUPPA JOE CAN'T HELP YOU HANDLE

Truly Important
Moments in Life
Should Be
Accompanied
by a

FULL
ORCHESTRAL
SCORE

**When Surrounded
by Bad Guys,
<u>Remember</u>:
They Live by
An Unspoken Code
Which Demands
That Even If
They Outnumber You
Twelve-to-One,
They Can
<u>Only</u>
Attack You
One at a Time.

Anyone With Billing Above The Title CANNOT Die

A MAN
IN
LOVE
IS

A

FOOL

...BUT A WOMAN IN LOVE HAS FOUND HER DESTINY!

Whenever
A Man
Proposes,
The Woman
Says
"YES!"

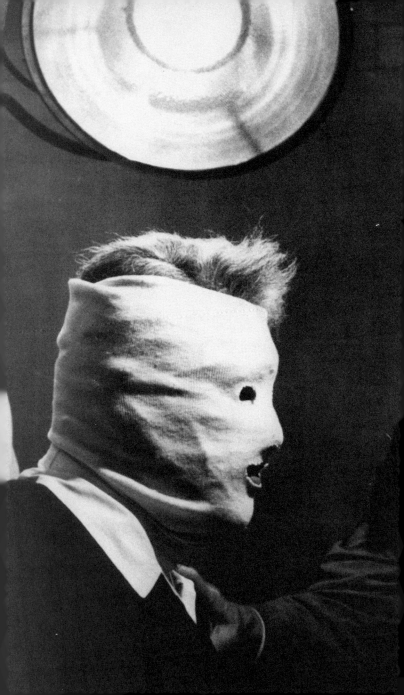

Serious Wounds
Need Only
Remain Bandaged
Until
The Audience
has had
Sufficient Time
To Forget
The Scene
in Which
The Injury
Occurred.

Whenever
You Find Yourself
at a
Major Crossroads
in Life,
Your Co-Stars'
Dialogue
Will Replay
in Your Head
...*With an Echo!*

In
Really Tense
Situations,
Foreign
Characters
Sometimes
Forget
Their
Accents.

Within Every Woman
Wearing Glasses
with
Her Hair Up in a Bun
Lurks
A Libidinous

Just Waiting
to be
Let Out

ONLY
REALLY
IMPORTANT
WOMEN
CAN
GET AWAY
WITH WEARING
REALLY
RIDICULOUS
HATS

The Earliest Warning Signs
of
A Brain Tumor
Include:
Squinting a Lot,
Complaining About
How Dark It Is
and
Constantly
Bumping into Furniture.

In
Serendipitous
Circumstances,
Two People
Who've Never
Met Before
Can Easily
Pull Off
An Intricately
Choreographed
Three-Minute
Dance Number.

WHEN PEOPLE
ARE NOT
AROUND,
FOREST ANIMALS
COMMUNICATE
BY SPEAKING,
SINGING SONGS
AND DOING
MUSICAL
NUMBERS

In The Proper
Romantic Setting,
One Man
with
One Guitar
Can Create The Sound
of an

Entire

Orchestra

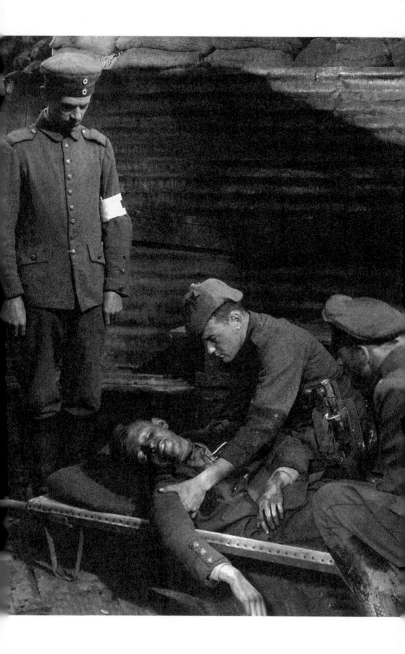

In Order To Motivate The Hero, His BEST BUDDY (Mother, Wife, Fiancée, Dog, Etc.) MUST DIE

AT AN
OPEN CASKET
FUNERAL,

IF
YOU LOOK
CLOSELY,
THE DEARLY
DEPARTED ONE
MAY STILL BE
BREATHING!

HEAVEN

Has an Endless
Supply
of
Harps,
Feathered Wings
and
Dry Ice

IT
ALWAYS
RAINS
AT
FUNERALS

EVERYTHING

WILL EVENTUALLY MAKE SENSE.

IF YOU DIE
UNDER THE RIGHT
CIRCUMSTANCES,
YOU CAN ALWAYS
BE BROUGHT BACK
FOR THE SEQUEL

All of
Life's Problems
Can Be Solved
BEFORE
The Final
Fade Out…

Every Movie Has A HAPPY ENDING.

**If Enough People
Don't Like
How
The Story
Turns Out,
The Ending
Can Be**

~~Re Wr~~ *Changed!*

PHOTO CREDITS

Page:

8   Buster Keaton in SHERLOCK, JR. ©1924 Metro

34   Karen Lynn Gorney and John Travolta in SATURDAY NIGHT FEVER ©1977
     Paramount Pictures

36   Ruby Keeler and Warner Baxter in 42nd STREET ©1933 Warner Bros.

40   Don Ameche in THE STORY OF ALEXANDER GRAHAM BELL ©1939 20th Century-Fox

48   Whoopi Goldberg in SISTER ACT ©1992 Touchstone Pictures

54   Lewis Stone and Mickey Rooney in THE COURTSHIP OF ANDY HARDY ©1942
     Metro-Goldwyn-Mayer

62   William Holden and Audrey Hepburn in PARIS WHEN IT SIZZLES ©1964
     Paramount Pictures

64   James Stewart in MR. SMITH GOES TO WASHINGTON ©1939 Columbia Pictures

76   Unknown Players in THE POTTERS AT HOME, ©1928 Vitaphone

80   Bruce Cabot (center) in FURY ©1936 Metro-Goldwyn-Mayer

86   Henry Fonda and Vera Miles in THE WRONG MAN ©1957 Warner Bros.

88   Edward G. Robinson in LITTLE CAESAR © 1930, Warner Bros.

94   Leo Genn in THE WOODEN HORSE ©1950 Wessex/British Lion

96   Burt Lancaster in BIRDMAN OF ALCATRAZ ©1962 United Artists

102 Publicity Still of Cecil B. DeMille © circa 1935 Paramount Pictures

106 Kirk Douglas and Unidentified Player in INDIAN FIGHTER ©1955
     Bryna Productions/United Artists

112 Jack Palance in SHANE ©1953 Paramount Pictures

120 Dwight Frye and Unidentified Player in HOT SANDS © circa 1930 Vitaphone

126 Dustin Hoffman and Anne Bancroft in THE GRADUATE ©1967 Embassy Pictures

146 Peter Lorre and Sydney Greenstreet in a Publicity Still © circa 1945 Warner Bros.

162 Deanna Durbin in 100 MEN AND A GIRL ©1937 Universal Pictures

186 Marilyn Monroe in HOW TO MARRY A MILLIONAIRE ©1953 20th Century-Fox

190 Bette Davis in DARK VICTORY ©1939 Warner Bros.

192 Fred Astaire and Cyd Charisse in THE BAND WAGON ©1953 Metro-Goldwyn-Mayer

202 Fred Astaire and Gene Kelly in ZIEGFELD FOLLIES OF 1946 ©1946
     Metro-Goldwyn-Mayer

204 Lana Turner and Sandra Dee in PORTRAIT IN BLACK ©1960 Universal International Pictures

ADDITIONAL PHOTOS

PHOTO BY BARBARA WILSON

ABOUT THE AUTHOR

In his 41 years on Planet Hollywood, John JB Wilson has seen, by his own estimation, more than 4,000 movies—many of them in his capacity as founder of The Golden Raspberry Award Foundation and creator of the annual Oscar parody *The RAZZIE Awards*, which have dis-honored worst achievements in film since 1980.

His twisted sense of humor and incurable cinemania result from a lifetime as a raving movie fan whose experiences include skipping school to sit in the bleachers awaiting the stars' arrivals at several 1960s Academy Awards ceremonies, staying up 'till all hours with his parents and brothers to watch 2 a.m. reruns of LOST HORIZON and SUNSET BOULEVARD, and working nights at a first-run movie theatre in posh Westwood Village while attending UCLA's prestigious Motion Picture/TV department by day.

Wilson now lives with his lovely wife Barbara (whom he met working at the movie theatre), three cats (named Nick and Nora Charles and Opie Taylor), three VCRs, a 359 volume film reference library and a collection of more than 1,357 video tapes, in an ever-more-crowded 800 square-foot house in the tinsel town suburb of Encino.